The Sheppard Family,

You are in our thoughts and prayers. Wishing you many happy years to come!

Sincerely,
Bill and Caryn Flaherty and family

SIMPLE

TRUTHS

By the Author

Small Graces
Letters to My Son
Neither Wolf nor Dog
Simple Truths
A Haunting Reverence

Edited by the Author

Native American Wisdom
The Soul of an Indian
The Wisdom of the Great Chiefs

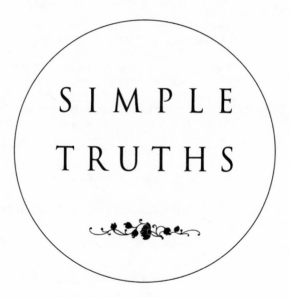

[KENT NERBURN]

SIMPLE TRUTHS

Clear & Gentle Guidance on the Big Issues in Life

14 Pamaron Way
Novato, California 94949

©1996 Kent Nerburn

Much of the material in this book is excerpted from
Letters to My Son, ©1993 Kent Nerburn

Cover Design: Nita Ybarra Design
Text Design & Typography: Linda Corwin

Library of Congress Cataloging-in-Publication Data

Nerburn, Kent, 1946 -
Simple truths : clear and gentle guidance
on the big issues in life / Kent Nerburn.
p.   cm.   ISBN 1-880032-92-9
(cloth : alk. paper)
1. Conduct of life. 2. Spiritual life. 3. Success.   I. Title.
BJ1581.2.N447   1996   96-5130
170'.44—dc20   CIP

First Printing, March 1996
Printed in the U.S.A. on acid-free paper
ISBN 1-880032-92-9
Distributed by Publishers Group West
10 9 8

In honored memory of my father,
Lloyd Nerburn,
who lived a life of simple truths.

Contents

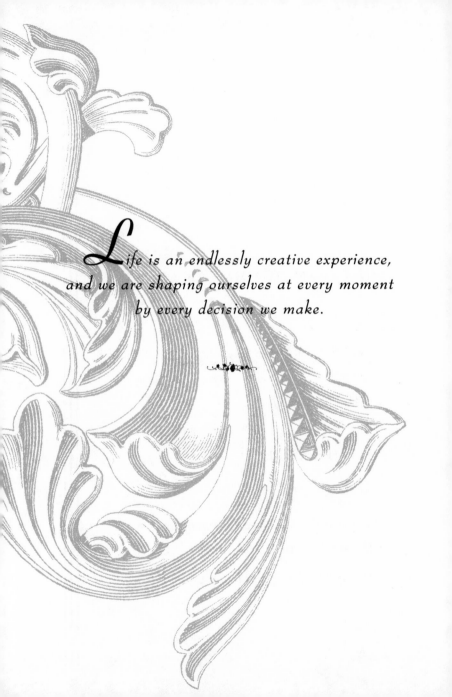

*L*ife is an endlessly creative experience,
and we are shaping ourselves at every moment
by every decision we make.

Introduction

The world is full enough of grand moralizing and private visions. The last thing I ever intended was to risk adding my voice to the long list of those involved in such endeavors.

Then, in midlife, everything changed. I was surprised with the birth of a child. I saw before me a person who would have to make his way through the tangle of life by such lights as he could find. It was, and is, incumbent upon me to guide him.

As I look around, I am concerned. The world is full of contrary visions, viewpoints, and recriminations. Our brightest dreams and our greatest fears are just over the horizon. Clear and measured voices are hard to find.

If I can offer something of value, it is this: a vision of life that acknowledges our human condition while remaining hopeful about our human potential; a voice that speaks with compassion and empathy about the world in which we live; and a viewpoint that seeks a common ground from which to survey the vast and confusing landscape before us.

We live in a time when it is hard to speak from the heart. The poetry of our spirits is silenced by the thoughts and cares of a thousand trivialities. This small book is my attempt to speak from the heart about some of life's biggest issues.

I offer it to you as both a father and a friend.

– KENT NERBURN

SIMPLE

TRUTHS

O_n
$\mathcal{E}ducation$
and
$\mathcal{L}earning$

Education is one of the great joys and solaces of life. It gives us a framework for understanding the world around us and a way to reach across time and space to touch the thoughts and feelings of others.

But education is more than schooling. It is a cast of mind, a willingness to see the world with an endless sense of curiosity and wonder.

If you would be truly educated, you must adopt this cast of mind. You must open yourself to the richness of your everyday experience — to your own emotions, to the movements of the heavens and the languages of birds, to the privations and successes of people in other lands and other times, to the artistry in the hands of the mechanic and the typist and the child. There is no limit to the learning that appears before us. It is enough to fill us each day a thousand times over.

The dilemma of how best to educate has always pivoted on the issue of freedom to explore versus the structured transmission of knowledge.

Some people believe that we learn best by wandering forth into an uncharted universe and making sense of the lessons that life provides.

Others believe that we learn best by being taught the most complete knowledge possible about a subject, then being sent forth to practice and use that knowledge.

Both ways have been tried with every possible

method and in every possible combination and balance.

If we find ourselves tempted to celebrate one approach over the other, we should remember the caution of the Chinese sage, Confucius, who told his followers, "Study without thinking and you are blind; think without studying and you are in danger."

Formal schooling is one way of gaining education, and it should not be underestimated. School, if it is good, imparts knowledge and a context for understanding the world around us. It opens us to ideas that we could never discover on our own, and makes us one with the life of the mind as it has been shaped by people and cultures that we could never meet in our own experience. It makes us part of a community of learners, and helps us give form and direction to the endless flow of experience that passes before us.

It is also a great frustration, because it often

seems irrelevant to the passions of our own interests and beliefs.

When you feel burdened by formal education, do not be quick to cast it aside. What is happening is a great surge in your growth and consciousness that is screaming out for immediate and total exploration.

You must remember that all other learners have traveled the same path. And though all true learners have felt this urge to strike out on their own, formal education, in its many shapes and guises, has been sought and revered by all people and all cultures at all times. It has a genius that is greater than your passions, and is abandoned at your own peril.

Still, formal education will not inform your spirit and make you full. So, along with knowledge, you must seek wisdom. Knowledge is multiple, wisdom is singular. Knowledge is words, wisdom is silent. Knowledge is standing outside, understanding what is seen, wisdom is standing at the center, knowing what is not seen. No person can be whole without both dimensions of learning.

There are many ways to seek wisdom. There is travel, there are masters, there is service. There is staring into the eyes of children and elders and lovers and strangers. There is sitting silently in one spot and there is being swept along in life's turbulent current. Life itself will grant you wisdom in ways you may neither understand nor choose.

It is up to you to be open to all these sources of wisdom and to embrace them with your whole heart.

So do not disparage the lessons of either the schooled or the unschooled.

Those who have less formal education may have learned some single thing more deeply, or they may have embarked early upon the search

for wisdom. In their uniqueness, they have dis-
covered something special about life, and it is
yours to experience if you are open to what they
have to teach.

Those who have devoted their life to formal
learning may have walked further along a path
than you can even imagine, and may be able to
lead you to a vista that will take your breath away,
if only you can overcome your boredom and
fatigue at the rigors of the search.

Remember the words of the musician who was
asked which was greater, knowledge or wisdom.
"Without knowledge," he answered, "I could not
play the violin. Without wisdom, I could not play
the music."

Place yourself among those who carry on their
lives with passion, and true learning will take
place, no matter how humble or exalted the set-
ting. But no matter what path you follow, do not
be ashamed of your learning. In some corner of

your life, you know more about something than anyone else on earth. The true measure of your education is not what you know, but how you share what you know with others.

O_n
W_{ork}

Choose your work carefully.

No matter how much you might believe that your work is nothing more than what you do to make money, your work makes you who you are, because it is where you put your time.

We are what we do, and the more we do it, the more we become it. By giving a job your time you are giving it your consciousness. Eventually it will fill your life with the reality that it presents.

So look beyond the superficial attractions of a particular job or profession. Consider what it will require you to do on a day-to-day, hour-to-hour, minute-to-minute basis. See if that is how you want to spend your time.

If it is not, your job will become your prison rather than the vehicle of your dreams. And a person without dreams is only half alive.

You should think of work as *vocation*, which comes from the Latin word for *calling*, which comes from the word for *voice*. In those meanings it touches on what work really should be — something that calls to you, that gives voice to who you are and what you want to say in the world.

If you find a vocation, embrace it. You have found a way to contribute to the world with love.

Finding a vocation is not always easy.

You can't really know what it is you want to do by thinking about it. You have to do it and see how it fits. You have to let the work take you over until it becomes you and you become it. Then you have to decide whether to embrace it or to abandon it.

There is no reason why a person can't abandon a job that does not fit and strike out into the unknown for something that lies closer to the heart. There is no reason why a person cannot have two, three, or more careers in the course of a life. No amount of security is worth the suffering of a life lived chained to a routine that has killed your dreams.

I once had a professor who dreamed of being a concert pianist. Fearing the possibility of failure, he went into academics where the work was secure and the money predictable. One day, when I was talking to him about my unhappiness in my graduate studies, he walked over and sat down at his piano. He played a beautiful glissando and then, abruptly, stopped. "Do what is in your heart," he said. "I really wanted to be a concert pianist. Now I spend every day wondering how good I might have been."

Find what it is that burns in your heart and do it. Choose a vocation, not a job, and your life will have meaning and your days will have peace.

O_n
$\mathcal{M}oney$

$\mathbf{M}$oney rules our lives.

You can rail against it. You can claim to be above it or indifferent to it. You can do all the moral and intellectual gymnastics that you will. But when all is said and done, money is at the very center of our existence. Yet money is not of central importance. It has nothing whatsoever to do with the lasting values that make life worth living.

This is one of our great dilemmas.

How are we to reconcile ourselves to something that is not important but is at the very center of our lives?

I have watched people with vast amounts of money who would not give away a nickel out of fear that they would be made poor, and poor people who always seemed to have enough to share with others. I have seen the gracious rich, the criminal poor, the hustler, and the saint. All of them have one thing in common: The way they deal with money is a result of how they think about money, not of how much money they have.

Money on its most basic level is a hard fact — either you have it or you don't. But on its emotional and psychological level it is purely a fiction. It becomes what you let it become.

Imagine two different people. The first builds his life around his desires. He has an internal accounting system that projects the amount of money he needs to meet his desires, and he feels he is poor unless he has that much.

On the basic level of money, this man feels poor unless he can fill in the distance between his present position and his fantasies with the money necessary to bring those fantasies to life. He may be a millionaire, but if his fantasies run into the billions, in his own mind he is poor.

Another person, who sees money as a simple tool of moving through life, will feel comfortable if she has a dollar more than she needs in her pocket, and positively rich if she has ten dollars more than she needs.

She has not built her happiness around desires, so she does not have to measure her money against those desires. She simply has an extra dollar she can spend any way she wants.

The difference between these two people does not lie in their actual wealth. It lies in their psychological relationship to money. They may have exactly the same amount of money — but one measures money against desires, the other measures it against needs.

People who measure their money against their desires will never be happy, because there is always another desire waiting to lure them. People who measure their money against their needs can gain control over their life by gaining control over their needs.

There are certain needs that have to be met. Even people who pare their financial needs to an absolute minimum cannot overcome the grinding oppression of not having enough to eat or not being able to clothe their family.

When you don't have enough to survive, money becomes the centerpiece of your life because you are obsessed with its absence, and your heart very quickly fills with desperation and anger.

If you find yourself filled with the anger and desperation of smothering poverty, you have to rise above it to communicate your hope. You have to reach inside yourself and find your sense of self-worth and your belief that you can and will do better. Then you have to reach out and communicate that belief.

The world is full of desperate people. Even people who want to help can give only so much. They will not respond to more than they see. If they see a hungry man, they will try to feed him. If they see an angry man, they will try to avoid him. If they see a promising man, they will try to help him fulfill his promise.

Show your promise, not your anger and desperation, and the hand of poverty will more readily release its grip on your life.

When it comes to defeating the desperation of poverty, your only real friend is work. Work — any work — rebuilds the sense of inner worth that desperation takes away. No matter how petty, work establishes the framework for growth and gives you a place to stand as you try to reach for something higher.

If the burden of poverty comes over you, do not look for money. Look for work. The money will follow, and you can begin to move money out of the center of your life and return it to its rightful place as a tool that helps you live a meaningful life.

Money can tyrannize the wealthy as easily as the poor. Even if you have no interest in money — if you want it only so you don't have to worry about it — at a certain point it becomes an abstraction that operates by abstract laws. It accumulates interest, you need to figure out how to invest it, you need to pay taxes according to how much you make, and it becomes a possession with a life of its own. You need to tend it with vigilance, and it soon becomes central in your mind, even though you thought that possessing it would set you free.

So how should you deal with money? There are no hard and fast rules. But there are some basic guidelines to keep in mind.

The first is this: It is as important to know how to be poor as it is to know how to be rich.

Financial well-being is nothing more than a balancing act on the back of circumstance. You can be thrown off at any time.

If you know how to be poor with dignity and grace, nothing short of massive financial disaster can disturb your peace of mind.

Knowing how to be poor means developing an unerring instinct for the difference between what is essential and what is only desirable. It means knowing how to take control of your life — how to repair and maintain the things around you, how to purchase wisely and well, how not to purchase at all when you do not have the means to do so, how to take joy in the simple pleasures in life.

It means not getting caught up in what is

lacking, but finding meaning in what you have. It means knowing how to live with style and creativity without basing your life on money.

If you learn to accept poverty when it comes, it will make you clearer and stronger and more self-reliant. It will make you more appreciative of the simple gifts of life. But you must learn to live by its rules and to embrace the life of limitations that it forces upon you.

A second guideline is this: Stay away from debt in your personal life. Debt, not poverty, is the greatest enemy of financial well-being and peace of mind.

There are massive forces arrayed in the world to tell you of the great benefits of debt. They will tell you that by borrowing you establish your legitimacy in the eyes of lenders. They will tell you that you can have tomorrow's pleasures at today's prices.

They will present arguments and inducements

that are convincing and seductive. They will dress debt up in a suit and call it credit. But it all comes down to the same thing: You have mortgaged your future to pay for your present, and this is something you don't ever want to do.

Debt can make you money because it allows you to invest when the opportunity presents itself. Debt can help you in the present and leave your problems for what you hope will be a better time in the future.

But debt defines your future, and when your future is defined, hope begins to die. You have committed your life to making money to pay for your past.

Stay away from debt if you can. There is no sadder sight than the person with dreams and promise whose eyes have dulled and whose days are spent pushing the heavy wheel of debt toward an endless horizon.

This is a third guideline: Money tends to move

away from those who try to hoard it, and toward those who share it.

If you are a hoarder, you live with a locked vault in your heart. Nothing can get in, nothing can get out. If you are a sharer, you bring out the sharer in others. Then money moves freely.

Money is like any other language through which people communicate. People who speak the same language tend to find each other. If you are one whose money speaks of protection and hoarding, you will find yourself involved with others whose money speaks the same language. You will be staring at each other with hooded eyes and closed fists and suspicion will be your common value.

If your money speaks of sharing, you will find yourself among people who want their money to speak the language of sharing, and your world will be filled with possibility.

A fourth guideline to keep in mind is that

money comes and goes. You must not be immobilized by the fear of losing it.

I often think of an old man who lives near us. He lives in near poverty and is a curmudgeonly sort. His livelihood is making doghouses. We live in a very poor part of the country where there is little money for people houses, much less doghouses. Yet this man insists on selling his doghouses for more than people around here can pay.

At one point I needed a doghouse. Unaware of his prices, I went over to see him. I told him how much I had. I was five dollars short. "My price is my price," he said, and slammed the door.

Now, when I drive by his house I see his yard crammed with doghouses. His house is falling down. His life is mired in poverty. But he will not change his price. He has established a value in his own mind and no one shares that value. His life cannot go forward until he frees himself from his conviction that he cannot take a loss. He will die surrounded by his doghouses, and they will be sold for five dollars apiece at a yard sale.

Learn from the old man. He is fixated on the doghouses, not on what they will enable him to do. Nothing should be worth more to you than its value in helping you live your life. If you are willing to slough off the past, even at a loss, you are keeping yourself free, and your world continues to grow. If you insist on holding to some abstract valuation, you are being held hostage by that possession, and you are trapped in a prison of your own devise.

No matter how you choose to deal with money, you need to keep one basic truth before you at all times: Money is nothing more than a commodity, an agreed-upon abstraction of exchange. It is the spirit of that exchange that animates money and gives it meaning. Great givers, rich and poor, use money to bring light into this world. Great hoarders, rich and poor, use money to close doors between us all.

Be a giver and a sharer. In some unexpected and unforeseeable fashion, all else will take care of itself.

O_n
$P_{ossessions}$

Most of our possessions arrive in our lives almost by accident. Gradually, like falling snow, they accumulate around us until they form the basis for our identity.

We do not intend this to happen. Most things we acquire are meant to increase our happiness and sense of fulfillment. But their uniqueness is quickly subsumed into the ordinariness of daily affairs.

We wake up one day and find ourselves surrounded by possessions that mean nothing to us. Our freedom is gone; our lightness of being is gone. In their place is a sense of responsibility and ownership. We have become curators of our own cluttered reality.

What has happened?

Unwittingly, we have allowed ourselves to be trapped by the thrill of the hunt. In our excitement we have forgotten that the pursuit of most possessions is nothing more than that — a pursuit — and have allowed ourselves to believe that our happiness would be increased by the next possession we acquire. But, in fact, our lives have slowly developed a sense of physical mass, and we are being bound to the earth like stones.

We must remember that most possessions are really butterflies that turn into caterpillars. They start with the wings of fantasy. We see them as freedom, as happiness. We believe they have the power to change our lives.

We pursue them with energy and excitement. When we finally get them, they give us a moment of elation; then, like an echo, a feeling of hollowness comes over us. The thrill of ownership begins to grow cold in our hands.

Still, swearing off possessions is not going to make us any clearer or wiser.

Unless we want to dedicate ourselves to some higher ascetic ideal, it will only make us obsessed with our own poverty, and neither the self-absorbed poor nor the self-absorbed rich are doing themselves or anyone else any good.

We need to find a true measure for our possessions so we can free ourselves from their weight without denying them their potential for good.

We must always remember that possessions have no inherent value. They become what we make them.

If they increase our capacity to give, they become something good. If they increase our focus on ourselves and become standards by which we measure other people, they become something bad.

When we seek a possession, we should ask ourselves if it will make us better people, more able to share, more willing to give, more capable of doing good in our daily lives. Possessions that increase our own sense of self-importance are empty in comparison to those that help us contribute something of value to the world.

Keep in mind that possessions are as likely to make you unhappy as they are to make you happy, because they define the limits of your life and keep you from the freedom of choice that comes with traveling light upon the earth.

They are chameleons that change from fantasies into responsibilities once you hold them in your hand, because they take your eye from the heavens and rivet it squarely on the earth.

If it is the thrill of pursuit you seek, recognize it. Embrace it and value it for the joy it gives you. But do not confuse the pursuit with the object being pursued.

And when the objects accumulate, do what you must to free yourself from their false importance. Give away what you don't use. Go on a long trip and travel lightly. Find a possession you value highly and give it to someone who would value it more. Do something to remind yourself that most of your possessions are nothing more than unimportant decorations on who you really are.

Listen to the quieter wisdom that says you will value your possessions more if you have fewer of them, and that you will find deeper meaning in human sharing than in the accumulation of goods.

If you build up possessions just as the logical outcome of pursuing your desires, you will lose your wings to fly.

On
Giving

Giving is a miracle that can transform the heaviest of hearts. Two people, who moments before lived in separate worlds of private concerns, suddenly meet each other over a simple act of sharing. The world expands, a moment of goodness is created, and something new comes into being where before there was nothing.

Too often we are blind to this everyday

miracle. We build our lives around accumulation — of money, of possessions, of status — as a way of protecting ourselves and our families from the vagaries of the world. Without thinking, we begin to see giving as an economic exchange — a sub- tracting of something from who and what we are — and we weigh it on the scales of self-interest.

But true giving is not an economic exchange, it is a generative act. It does not subtract from what we have; it multiplies the effect we can have in the world.

Many people tend to think of giving only in terms of grand gestures. They miss the simple openings of the heart that can be practiced any- where with almost anyone.

We can say hello to someone everybody ignores. We can offer to help a neighbor. We can buy a bouquet of flowers and take it to a nursing home, or spend an extra minute talking to some- one who needs our time.

We can take ten dollars out of our pocket and give it to someone on the street. No praise, no hushed tones of holy generosity. Just give, smile, and walk away.

If you perform these simple acts, little by little you will start to understand the miracle of giving. You will begin to see the unprotected human heart and the honest smiles of human happiness. You will start to feel what is common among us, not what separates and differentiates us.

Before long you will discover that you have the power to create joy and happiness by your simplest gestures of caring and compassion. You will see that you have the power to unlock the goodness in other people's hearts by sharing the goodness in yours.

And, most of all, you will find the other givers. No matter where you live or where you travel, whether you speak their language or know their names, you will know them by their small acts, and they will recognize you by yours. You will become part of the community of humanity that trusts and shares and dares to reveal the softness of its heart.

Once you become a giver you will never be alone.

On Travel

Wanderlust, the urge for adventure, the desire to know what is over the next hill, are like echoes in the backs of our minds that speak of sounds not quite heard and places not quite seen.

You should listen to these echoes. Take the chances and follow the voices that call you to distant places. Live, if only for a short time, the life of a traveler. It is a life you will always cherish and never forget.

The magic of travel is that you leave your home secure in your own knowledge and identity, but as you travel, the world in all its richness intervenes. You meet people you could not invent; you see scenes you could not imagine. Your own world, which was so large as to consume your whole life, becomes smaller and smaller until it is only one tiny dot in space and time. You return a different person.

Travel doesn't have to be to some dreamlike and foreign destination. It can take you on an evening stroll through a distant forest or to a park bench in a town a hundred miles from your home. What matters is that you have left the comfort of the familiar and opened yourself to a world that is totally apart from your own.

Many people don't want to be travelers. They would rather be tourists, flitting over the surface of other people's lives while never really leaving their own. They try to bring their world with them wherever they go, or try to recreate the world they left. They do not want to risk the security of their own understanding and see how small and limited their experiences really are.

To be a real traveler, you must be willing to give yourself over to the moment and take yourself out of the center of your universe. You must believe totally in the lives of the people and the places where you find yourself.

Become part of the fabric of their everyday lives. Embrace them rather than judge them, and you will find that the beauty in their lives and their world will become part of yours. When you move on you will have grown. You will realize that the possibilities of life in this world are endless, and that beneath our differences of language and culture we all share the same dream of loving and being loved, of having a life with more joy than sorrow.

Travel is not as romantic and exotic as you imagine it. The familiar will always call. Your sense of rootlessness will not give you rest.

You may wake one day and find that you have become a runner who uses travel as an escape from the problems and complications of trying to build something with your life. You may find that you have stayed away one hour or one day or one month too long, and that you no longer belong anywhere or to anyone. You may find that you have been caught by the lure of the road and that you are a slave to dissatisfaction with any life that forces you to stay in one place.

But how much worse is it to be someone whose dreams have been buried beneath the routines of life and who no longer has an interest in looking beyond the horizon?

If we don't offer ourselves to the unknown, our senses dull. Our world becomes small and we lose our sense of wonder. Our eyes don't lift to the horizon; we don't hear the sounds around us. The edge is off our experience and we pass our days in a routine that is both comfortable and limiting. We wake up one day and find that we have lost our dreams in order to protect our days.

Travel, no matter how humble, will etch new elements in your character. You will know the cutting moments of life where fear meets adventure and loneliness meets exhilaration. You will know what it means to push forward when you want to turn back.

And when you have tragedies or great changes in your life, you will understand that there are a thousand, a million ways to live, and that your life will go on to something new and different and every bit as worthy as the life you are leaving behind.

Because I have traveled, I can see other universes in the eyes of strangers. I know what parts of me I cannot deny and what parts of me are simply choices that I make. I know the blessings of my own table and the warmth of my own bed. I know how much of life is pure chance, and how great a gift I have been given simply to be who I am.

When I am old, and my body has begun to fail me, my memories will be waiting for me. They will lift me and carry me over mountains and oceans. I will hold them and turn them and watch them catch the sunlight as they come alive once more in my imagination. I will be rich and I will be at peace.

I want you to have that peace, too.

Take the chances a traveler has to take. In the end you will be so much richer, so much stronger, so much clearer, so much happier, and so much a better person that all the risk and hardship will seem like nothing compared to the knowledge and wisdom you have gained.

On
Loneliness
and
Solitude

You should spend time alone. Not just minutes and hours, but days, and if the opportunity presents itself, weeks.

Time spent alone returns to you a hundredfold, because it is the proving ground of the spirit. You quickly find out if you are at peace with yourself, or if the meaning of your life is found only in the superficial affairs of the day. If it is in the superficial affairs of the day, time spent alone will throw you back upon yourself in a way that will make you grow in wisdom and inner strength.

We can easily fill our days with activity. We buy, we sell, we move from place to place. There is always more to be done, always a way to keep from staring into the still pool where life is more than the chatter of the small affairs of the mind.

If we are not careful, we begin to mistake this activity for meaning. We turn our lives into a series of tasks that can occupy all the hours of the clock and still leave us breathless with our sense of work left undone.

And always there is work undone. We will die with work undone. The labors of life are endless. Better that you should accept the rhythms of life and know that there are times when you need to stop to draw a breath, no matter how great the labors are before you.

For many people, solitude is just a poet's word for being alone. But being alone, in itself, is nothing. It can be a breeding ground of loneliness as easily as a source of solitude.

Solitude is a condition of peace that stands in direct opposition to loneliness. Loneliness is like sitting in an empty room and being aware of the space around you. It is a condition of separateness. Solitude is becoming one with the space around you. It is a condition of union.

Loneliness is small, solitude is large. Loneliness closes in around you; solitude expands toward the infinite. Loneliness has its roots in words, in an internal conversation that nobody answers; solitude has its roots in the great silence of eternity.

Most people fear being alone because they understand only loneliness. Their understanding begins at the self, and they are comfortable only as long as they are at the center of their understanding. Solitude is about getting the "I" out of the center of our thoughts so that other parts of life can be experienced in their fullness. It is about abandoning the self as the focus of understanding, and giving ourselves over to the great flowing fabric of the universe.

Though this may sound mystical and abstract, the universe has an eternal hum that runs beyond our individual birth and death. It is a hum that is hard to hear through the louder and closer noise of our daily lives. It is the unity that transcends us all and, as much as possible, reconciles us to the reality and inevitability of our deaths. It makes us part of something larger. In solitude alone do we become part of this great eternal sound.

Nature is the clearest source of solitude. The greatness of nature can overwhelm the insignificant chatter by which we measure most of our days. If you have the wisdom and the courage to go to nature alone, the larger rhythms, the eternal hum, will make itself known all the sooner. When you have found it, it will always be there for you. The peace without will become the peace within, and you will be able to return to it in your heart wherever you find yourself.

For most of us, the search involves a grinding of the gears as we slow from hurried to quiet to still to peaceful. But it is worth the struggle.

Slowly, inexorably, we emerge into the ultimate quiet of solitude. We are in a place where we are beyond thoughts — where we hear each sound and feel each heartbeat; where we are present to each change of sunlight on the earth around us, and we live in the awareness of the ongoing presence of life.

In this awareness the whole world changes. A tree ceases to be an object and becomes a living thing. We can smell its richness, hear its rustlings, sense its rhythms as it carries on its endless dance with the wind.

In solitude silence becomes a symphony. Time changes from a series of moments strung together into a seamless motion riding on the rhythms of the stars. Loneliness is banished, solitude is in full flower, and we are one with the pulse of life and the flow of time.

The awareness we experience in solitude is priceless for the peace it can give. It is also the key to true loving in our relationships. When we have a part of ourselves that is firm, confident, and alone, we don't need another person to fill us. We know that we have private spaces full of goodness and self-worth, and we grant the same to those we love. We do not try to pry into every corner of their lives or to fill the emptiness inside us with their presence.

As always, look at the world around you. The mountain is not restless in its aloneness. The hawk tracing circles in the sky is not longing for union with the sun. They exist in the perfect peace of an eternal present, and that is the peace that one finds only in solitude. Find this peace in yourself, and you will never know another moment of loneliness in your life.

O_n
$\mathcal{L}ove$

It is a mystery why we fall in love. It is a mystery how it happens. It is a mystery when it comes. It is a mystery why some loves grow and it is a mystery why some loves fail. You can analyze this mystery and look for reasons and causes, but you will never do any more than take the life out of the experience.

Love is more than the sum of the interests and attractions and commonalities that two people share. And just as life itself is a gift that comes and goes in its time, the coming of love must be taken as an unfathomable gift that cannot be questioned in its ways.

Too often, when love comes to people, they try to grasp the love and hold it to them, refusing to see that it is a gift freely given and a gift that just as freely moves away. When they fall out of love, or the person they love feels the spirit of love leaving, they try desperately to reclaim the love that is lost rather than accepting the gift for what it was.

They want answers where there are no answers. They want to know what is wrong with them, or they try to get their lover to change, thinking that if some small thing were different love would bloom again. They blame their circumstances. They blame each other. They try anything to give meaning to what has happened. But there is no meaning beyond the love itself, and until they accept its own mysterious ways they live in a sea of misery.

You need to treat what love brings you with kindness. If you find yourself in love with someone who does not love you, be gentle with yourself. There is nothing wrong with you. Love just didn't choose to rest in the other person's heart.

If you find someone else in love with you toward whom you feel no love, feel honored that love came and called at your door, but gently refuse the gift you cannot return. Do not take advantage, do not cause pain. How you deal with love is how love will deal with you, and all our hearts feel the same pains and joys, even if our lives and ways are very different.

If you fall in love with another who falls in love with you, and then love chooses to leave, do not try to reclaim it or to assess blame. Let it go. There is a reason and there is a meaning. You will know it in time, but time itself will choose the moment.

Remember this and keep it in your heart. You

don't choose love. Love chooses you. All you can really do is accept it for all its mystery when it comes into your life. Feel the way it fills you to overflowing, then reach out and give it away. Give it back to the person who brought it to you. Give it to others who seem poor in spirit. Give it to the world around you in any way you can.

Love has its own time, its own season, and its own reasons for coming and going. You cannot bribe it or coerce it or reason it into staying. If it chooses to leave, from your heart or from the heart of your lover, there is nothing you can do and nothing you should do. Be glad that it came to live for a moment in your life. If you keep your heart open, it will surely come again.

On Marriage

Sometimes marriage seems easier to understand for what it cuts out of our lives than for what it makes possible within our lives. When I was younger this fear immobilized me. I did not want to make a mistake.

I saw my friends getting married for reasons of social acceptability, or sexual fervor, or just because they thought it was the logical thing to do. Then I watched as they and their partners became embittered and petty in their dealings with each other.

I looked at older couples and saw, at best, mutual toleration. I imagined a lifetime of love-less nights and bickering days and could not imagine subjecting myself or someone else to such a fate.

On rare occasions, I would see old couples who somehow seemed to glow in each other's presence. They seemed really in love, not just dependent upon each other and tolerant of each other's foibles. It was an astounding sight, and it seemed impossible. How, I asked myself, can they have survived so many years of sameness, so much irritation at the other's habits? What keeps love alive in them, when most of us seem unable to even stay together, much less love each other?

The central secret seems to be in choosing well. There is something to the claim of fundamental compatibility. Good people can create a bad relationship, even though they both dearly want the relationship to succeed. It is important to find someone with whom you can create a good relationship from the outset.

Unfortunately, it is hard to see clearly in the early stages of a relationship. Sexual attraction blinds you to the thousands of little things by which relationships eventually survive or fail. You need to find a way to see beyond this initial overwhelming physical fascination.

Some people choose to involve themselves sexually and ride out the most heated period of sexual attraction in order to see what is on the other side. This can work, but it can also leave a trail of wounded hearts. Others deny the sexual altogether in an attempt to get to know each other apart from their sexuality. But they cannot see clearly, because the presence of unfulfilled sexual desire looms so large that it keeps them from having any normal perception of what life would be like together.

Truly fortunate partners manage to become longtime friends before they realize they are attracted to each other. They get to know each other's laughs, passions, sadnesses, and fears. They see each other at their worst and at their best. They share time together before they get swept up into the entangling intimacy of their sexuality.

Laughter is one clue to compatibility. It tells you how much you will enjoy each other's company over the long term. If your laughter together is good and healthy, and not at the expense of others, then you have a healthy relationship to the world.

Laughter is the child of surprise. If you can make each other laugh, you can always surprise each other. If you can always surprise each other, you can always keep the world around you new.

Beware of a relationship in which there is no laughter. Even the most intimate relationships based only on seriousness have a tendency to turn dour. Over time, sharing a common serious viewpoint on the world tends to turn you against those who do not share the same viewpoint, and your relationship can become based on being critical together.

Look for a partner who deals with the world in a way you respect. When two people first get together, they tend to see their relationship as existing only in the space between the two of them. They find each other endlessly fascinating, and the overwhelming power of the emotions they are sharing blinds them to the outside world. As the relationship ages and grows, the outside world becomes important again. If your partner treats people or circumstances in a way you can't accept, you will inevitably come to grief. If you do not respect the way you each deal with the world around you, eventually the two of you will not respect each other.

Look also at how your partner confronts the mysteries of life. We live on the cusp of poetry and practicality, and the real life of the heart resides within the poetic. If one of you is deeply affected by the mystery of the unseen in life and relationships, while the other is drawn only to the literal and practical, you must take care that the distance does not become an unbridgeable chasm that leaves you each feeling isolated and misunderstood.

Take the time to choose a partner carefully and well. Then the real miracle of marriage can take place in your life. Miracle is a powerful word, and I choose it carefully. But there is a miracle in marriage — the miracle of transformation.

Transformation is one of the most common events of nature. The seed becomes the flower. The cocoon becomes the butterfly. Winter becomes spring and love becomes a child.

Marriage is a transformation we choose to make. Our love is planted like a seed, and in time

it begins to flower. We cannot know the flower
that will bloom, but we can be sure that a bloom
will come. If we have chosen carefully and wisely,
the bloom will be good. If we have chosen poorly
or for the wrong reason, or we do not tend our
marriage with care, then the bloom will be flawed.

If you believe in your heart that you have found
someone with whom you are able to grow, if you
have sufficient faith that you can resist the endless
attraction of the road not taken and the partner
not chosen, if you have the strength to embrace
the cycles and seasons that your love will experience, then you may be ready to seek the miracle
that marriage offers. If not, then wait. The easy
grace of a marriage well made is worth your
patience.

On
Parenthood

There is little that is perfect in our lives. We seek the perfect lover, the perfect home, the perfect occupation. But always there is the lure of the unknown, the shadow of the path not chosen.

But there is one place where perfection of the heart is given to us in all its fullness — parenthood. When you look upon a child you have been given, there are no limitations and reservations. You are looking with a perfect love.

This is only natural. A child is born with a perfect love and dependence on its parents. In the perfection of its love, it calls forth the perfection of yours. In its innocence, it opens up a place of innocence in you. Something pure is communicated that can never be understood by those who have never looked into the eyes of an infant whose very survival is in their hands.

Along with the gift of purity of heart, a child gives you a gift of understanding.

When you experience parenthood, the whole world remakes itself before your eyes. Nature aligns itself. You understand your parents more and honor them more for the love they gave and the struggles they had. You see your own imperfections cast in high relief, because you know how much you want to do things right, and how hard it is to know what it is you should do. You feel the unity of generations cascading into generations from the beginning of time. You feel something in the world that is more important than yourself.

Your life suddenly becomes centered. Your own failings are cast in high relief, but so are your own strengths. You know what it is that you believe in and must pass along.

If you have a chance at parenthood, look upon it with a sense of mystery and awe. You are given the joy of watching life afresh, and the chance to help another being take flight into the richness and mystery of life. The very clay of which our world is made is, for a brief moment, placed in your hands.

Do not take this responsibility lightly.

When a child comes into your life, you must take care to give it family, however you define it, and history, and community. For the child learns of life from its context.

You must offer your highest vision of good, and a sense of moral purpose, and a healthy vision of the world outside.

Above all, you must be prepared to give your child time. For time alone shapes with silent hands. And you will never know when your child will choose to fly, if not in body, at least in mind and spirit, and move away from the life you have set out for it. When this day comes, the time you have given will be the only true measure of your influence, and from that day forward, it will be you who will long for the gift of time from your child.

So approach parenthood cautiously.

You need not fear it as a loss of freedom. In the bondage to a child you will find a freedom you never imagined. But neither should you seek parenthood as a way to fill an emptiness in your life. A child will hold a mirror to your life, and you will find your emptiness visited in some unimagined form upon the child itself.

Parenthood, above all else in life, requires wholeness. It is the placing of your entire life, with all its skills, all its beliefs, all its weaknesses, and all its strengths, before a child whose very being is shaped by each moment in your presence. If you have tended that presence well, and brought it to a form with which you are at peace, you can enter into parenthood with confidence and joy. If not, you should wait.

A child, whether of your blood or someone else's, whether healthy or ill, whether beautiful or misshapen, is one of life's greatest miracles. It opens your world into a new sunlight and is a gift greater than a dream. Be sure you are ready to receive it and honor it before you bring it into your life.

O_n
$Strength$

We each have a different kind of strength. Some of us are able to persevere against hopeless odds. Some are able to see light in a world of darkness. Some are able to give selflessly with no thought of return, while others are able to bring a sense of importance into the hearts of those around them.

But no matter how we exhibit strength, its truest measure is the calm and certain conviction with which it causes us to act. It is the ability to discern the path with heart, and follow it even when at the moment we might wish to be doing something else.

True strength is not about force, but about conviction. It lives at the center of belief where fear and uncertainty cannot gain a foothold. Its opposite is not cowardice and fear, but confusion, lack of clarity, and lack of sound intention.

True strength does not require an adversary and does not see itself as noble or heroic. It simply does what it must without praise or need of recognition.

A person who can quietly stay at home and care for an ailing parent is as strong as a person who can climb a mountain. A person who can stand up for a principle is as strong as a person who can fend off an army. They simply have quieter, less dramatic, kinds of strength.

True strength does not magnify others'

weaknesses. It makes others stronger. If someone's strength makes others feel weaker, it is merely domination, and that is no strength at all.

Take care to find your own true strength. Nurture it. Develop it. Share it with those around you. Let it become a light for those who are living in darkness.

Remember, strength based in force is a strength people fear. Strength based in love is a strength people crave.

On
Tragedy
and
Suffering

Tragedy and suffering will come to you. You cannot insulate yourself from them. You cannot avoid them. They come in their own season and in their own time. When they come, they will overwhelm you and immobilize you.

When all is going well, our world is a small, controlled experience bounded by our daily rituals and activities. When

85

tragedy and suffering come swooping in, they shatter our tiny boundaries and break our world into pieces.

For a time we are living inside a scream where there seems to be no exit, only echoes. The small cares that seemed so important yesterday seem like nothing, and our daily concerns become petty and irrelevant. When we finally reclaim ourselves, as we ultimately do, we are changed.

We have been carried into a larger realm where we see what is truly important, and it is our responsibility to carry that knowledge back into our daily lives. It is our chance to think life afresh.

How you respond to tragedy and suffering is one true measure of your strength. You need to see those moments as moments of growth. You need to look upon them as gifts to help you reclaim what is important in your life.

The human being is a surprisingly resilient

organism. We impel toward health, not sickness. Your spirit, as surely as your body, will try to heal.

The question you must ask yourself is not if you will heal, but how. Grief and pain have their own duration, and when they begin to pass, you must take care to guide the shape of the new being you are to become.

So you should not fear tragedy and suffering. Like love, they make you more a part of the human family. From them can come your greatest creativity. They are the fire that burns you pure.

The
Spiritual
Journey

We are all born with a belief in God. It may not have a name or a face. We may not even see it as God. But it is there.

It is the sense that comes over us as we stare into the starlit sky, or watch the last fiery rays of an evening sunset. It is the morning shiver as we wake on a beautiful day and smell a richness in the air that we know and love from somewhere we can't quite recall. It is the mystery behind the beginning of time and beyond the limits of space. It is a sense of otherness that brings alive something deep in our hearts.

Some people will tell you that there is no God. They will claim that God is a crutch for people who can't face reality, a fairy tale for people who need myths in their lives. They will argue for rational explanations for the origin of the universe and scientific explanations of the perfect movements of nature. They will point to evil and injustice in the world, and cite examples of religion being used to start wars or to hurt people of different beliefs.

You cannot argue with these people, nor should you. These are the people the Chinese philosopher Chuang Tzu spoke about when he said, "A frog in a well cannot be talked to about the sea."

If you have any sense of the mystery of the universe around you, you are hearing the murmur of the sea. Your task is to leave the well, to step out into the sun, and to set out for the sea. Leave the arguing to those who wish to discuss the size and shape of the walls that close them in.

If you hear the call of the distant sea, do not be turned away by the naivetés and contradictions of the beliefs around you. There are many paths, and the sea looks different from each of them. Your task is not to judge the paths of others, but to find a path that will lead you ever closer to the murmurings that you hear in your heart.

Begin by accepting where you are.

We all have special gifts of character. Some of us are blessed with compassion; others, laughter; others, a power of self-discipline. Some of us are filled with the beauty of people, others with the beauty of nature. Some of us have a keen sense of the injustices in life; others are drawn to celebrate the goodness around us.

These are all starting points, because they are all places of belief. You must find the gift that you have — the source of your belief — and discover a way to cultivate that gift.

If you come upon a tradition that seems to give voice to the music of your spirit, do not be afraid to follow. Religious traditions exist because they give voice to fundamental spiritual truths that many people share.

They offer a path to the sea that has been taken before, and their footsteps are well marked for those who choose to follow.

If you find a tradition that engages your spirit, give yourself to it with your whole heart. Read its texts. Participate in its rituals. Give yourself over to its ways of spiritual formation.

If, however, you find that your faith in God is something silent and personal to be found in the solitude of your own heart, do not be afraid to embark upon that path. Seek out the wisdom of the mystics and the visionaries who met their God face to face, and cultivate the habits of the heart that will allow you to grow closer to the experience of God every day.

Spiritual growth is honed and perfected only through practice. Like an instrument, it must be played. Like a path, it must be walked. Whether through prayer or meditation or worship or good works, you must move yourself in the direction of spiritual betterment. Spiritual understanding never becomes deep unless you subject yourself to the spiritual discipline of practicing your belief.

There will be times when you will feel you have lost your way. You will be too tired to go on, or other things will seem more important. Maybe you will start to feel that your belief was just a momentary enthusiasm. Maybe you will feel a growing meanness of spirit. Maybe you just won't care.

Don't be too hard on yourself when this happens. Your whole life is a spiritual journey, and you will find yourself in arid lands as well as in lands rich in possibility. Just be certain to continue to push forward. A few more steps and you will once again hear the call of the great waters.

Most of all, have faith in your path. Follow it as you can; change it if you must. But do not give up the search for the sea. As you get closer, the murmur gets louder, and your certainty of its existence will grow. You may not find yourself on the path you expected, but you will be on a path nevertheless.

Do not refuse to seek God because you cannot find the one truth. We live in a pluralistic world, and only the most hard-headed refuse to accept the fact that truth — whether spiritual, cultural, political, or otherwise — is given to different people in different ways.

Find the path that glows like a sunlit day, rich in remembered scents and promises. Then follow. Only a fool refuses to walk in the sunlight because he cannot see the shape of the sun.

O_n
$\mathcal{T}he$
$\mathcal{E}lders$

$\mathbf{Y}$our heart is revealed by the way you treat elders.

Like children, the elders are a burden. But unlike children, they offer no hope or promise. They are a weight and an encumbrance and a mirror of our own mortality. It takes a person of great heart to see past this fact to the wisdom elders have to offer, and to serve them out of gratitude for the life they have passed on to us.

Having gratitude for our elders is not easy in this culture. We have lost a feel for them. They are a sad, gray presence hidden behind clumsy phrases like "the elderly," "senior citizens," and "retired persons." They are tolerated out of guilt, feared for the burden they represent, or shunted aside into irrelevance. They are not loved and honored and sought out for the wisdom that their years have given them.

Even if theirs was the simplest, most limited, most ordinary of lives, the elders saw the world into which you have come. No other past generation is as close to yours; no other life so near in time. Their stories have the blood of your life running through them. You will never be so near to the world that gave birth to you as you are when speaking to them. For that and that alone you should honor and revere them and give them your ear. You are bonded in time.

 B ut more than that, the elders offer a glimpse into your own future. They were you and you will be them. You carry the seeds of your old age in you at this very moment, and they hear the echoes of their younger years each time they are in your presence.

Each touch you have with them makes you wiser in ways you cannot imagine.

 S till, many old people are not pleasant. They are as filled with themselves and their own concerns as are the very young. They ask you to think about their needs and feelings with little or no concern for yours.

When you meet such elders, do not be blinded by their unpleasantness. Like young children, they are dependent on the world around them, and they very often fear the loss of their own importance. They face the uncertainty of death and are often embittered that the world they worked so hard to create is being discarded by the generations now in power. Their bodies are giving out on them. They increasingly find themselves surrounded only by people their own age, because they know that the young would rather be apart from them. They often live in memories.

Look past these surface behaviors. Look to the person, not to the infirmities and idiosyncrasies. When you are tired or ill, or full of anger and pain, you, too, may not be pleasant. For many elders these are the conditions of their lives. But beneath the surface of their actions is a level of insight that only age can teach.

Avoid the pitfall of pity when dealing with the elders. Too many people, under the guise of caring, patronize and demean the very old by treating them like children. They speak to them loudly, or as if they were simpletons. They interpret the elder's concern for the small details of life as a return to the infantile. In actions and in manner they strip the elders of the very respect they claim to be giving them.

Such behavior holds up mirrors in which the elders must see their infirmity, not mirrors in which they can see their humanity. True caring and respect serve the weakness, but mirror only the humanity and the strength. Caring and respect listen, laugh, and even challenge. They assume that the words and actions of the elders are to be taken seriously.

Even in their infirmity, elders seek and value their dignity. They want, above all else, to feel that their lives are still valued, and that the world they made and the knowledge they gained are not being cast aside.

So love the elders. Honor them. Go to them with a pure heart, unblinded by notions of false reverence or obligation, and unaffected by self-serving feelings of pity. Listen to them. Observe them like a far-off country that you will someday visit, and learn the lessons that they have to teach.

If you can honor and respect them, and allow them to share the fruits of their experience, however simple those fruits might be, you will gain a gift you can get nowhere else.

You will gain the knowledge of your past, and the wisdom to understand your future.

O_n
$\mathcal{D}eath$

$\mathbf{D}$eath is our common mystery. Like birth and love, it is a bond that unites us all. Yet none of us can know for certain what it contains or what it portends.

We have glimpses from those who have experienced clinical death and returned to tell us what they saw. We have promises from all faiths and religions. However, we all must meet death alone, so it remains the great private preparation for each of us.

Many years ago I was present at a total eclipse of the sun.

I climbed to the crown of a high hill and sat down facing the growing morning light. Birds were singing. Cows and horses grazed on the hillside. As the moment came, and the moon began to carve away the sun, the earth became inexpressibly still. The winds ceased; the birds fell silent. The cows sank to their knees and the horses bowed their heads. Soon only the ghostly corona of the hidden sun remained to cast a fragile light on the dark and silent earth.

In that moment, something momentous happened. I lost my fear of death. The light of the sun had been taken from me and the world I knew had been cast into a great darkness. But there was no sense of terror; no sense of fear. The self was annihilated, but it was an annihilation into oneness.

I can't put a name to what was shown me in that moment. It was too far beyond the human for me to understand. But I do know that it had to do with death, and that I was swept up into the greatest peace that I have ever known, a peace that surpassed all understanding. I accepted it like the tranquil embrace of a long-sought sleep.

If that moment on the hillside contained truth — and I think it did — we do death no justice by measuring it against ourselves. We are too small; it is too great. What we fear is only the loss of self, and the self knows eternity like a shadow knows the sun.

So, fear dying if you must. It takes from us the only life we know, and that is a worthy loss to mourn. But do not fear death. It is something too great to celebrate, too great to fear. Either it brings us to a judgment, so it is ours to control by the kind of life we live, or it annihilates us into the great rhythm of nature, and we join the eternal peace of the revolving heavens.

In the brief moment when I stood on that hill

while the earth's light went out, I felt no indifference and no sense of loss. Instead I felt an unutterable sense of gain, a shattering of all my own boundaries into an overwhelming sense of peace. I was part of a great harmony.

We should embrace our dying as a momentary passage into that harmony. Perhaps we cannot hear that harmony now. Perhaps we even hear it as a vast and empty silence. But that vastness is not empty; it is a presence. Even in the greatest places, the silence has a sound.

Epilogue

Embracing the Mystery

When all the words have been written, and all the phrases have been spoken, the great mystery of life will still remain. We may map the terrains of our lives, measure the farthest reaches of the universe, but no amount of searching will ever reveal for certain whether we are all children of chance or part of a great design.

And who among us would have it otherwise? Who would wish to take the mystery out of the experience of looking into a new-born infant's eyes? Who would not feel in violation of something great if we had knowledge of what has departed when we stare into the face of one who has died? These are the events that make us human, that define the distance between us and the stars.

Still, this life is not easy. Much of its mystery is darkness. Tragedies occur, injustices exist. Bad things befall good people and sufferings are visited upon the innocent. To live we must take the lives of other species, to survive we must leave some of our brothers and sisters by the side of the road. We are prisoners of time, victims of biology, hostages of our own capacity to dream.

At times it all seems too much, impossible to accept.

We must stand against this. The world is a great and mysterious place, and it contains within it all the possibilities that our hearts can conceive. If we incline our hearts toward the darkness, we will see the darkness. If we incline them toward the light, we will see the light.

Life is but a dream we renew each day. It is up to us to infuse this dream with light, and to cultivate, as best as we are able, the ways and habits of love.

Those of great heart have always known this. They have understood that, as honorable as it is to see wrong and to try to correct it, a life well lived must somehow celebrate the promise that life provides. The darkness at the limits of our knowledge — the darkness that sometimes seems to surround us — is merely a way to make us reach beyond certainty, to make our lives a witness to hope, a testimony to possibility, an urge toward the best and the most honorable impulses that our hearts can conceive.

It is not hard. There is in each of us, no matter how humble, a capacity for love. Even if our lives have not taken the course we had envisioned, even if we are less than the shape of our dreams, we are part of the human family. Somewhere, in the most inconsequential corners of our lives, is the opportunity for love.

If I am blind, I can run my hand across the back of a shell and celebrate beauty. If I have no legs, I can sit in quiet wonder before the restless murmurs of the sea. If I am wounded in spirit, I can reach out my hand to those who are hurting. If I am lonely, I can go among those who are desperate for love. There is no tragedy or injustice so great, no life so small and inconsequential, that we cannot bear witness to the light in the quiet acts and hidden moments of our days.

And who can say which of these acts and moments will make a difference? The universe is a vast and magical membrane of meaning, stretching across time and space, and it is not given us to know her secrets and her ways. Perhaps we were placed here to meet the challenge of a single moment; perhaps the touch we make will cause the touch that will change the world.

When we come to the end of our journey, and the issues that so concerned us recede from us like the day before the coming night, it will be these small touches — the child we have helped, the garden we have planted, the meal we have prepared when we were too weary to do so — that will become our legacy to the universe.

If we have played our part well — offering love where it was needed, strength and caring where it was lacking; if we have tended the earth and its creatures with a sense of humble stewardship — we will have done enough. We may pass quietly, and rest gently in the knowledge that we have left the world a little warmer, a little kinder, a little richer in love. Though our moment was brief, and our part small, somewhere, in the fullness of time, our acts will bear fruit, and the earth will raise up a bit of goodness in our memory.

It is a small legacy, perhaps, but a legacy nonetheless. Somewhere, between a baby's cry and the distant brightness of a star, the mystery was alive in us for a moment. It was our privilege to feel its presence, and to have the chance to pass it on.

Acknowledgments

A book is the sum of all that you are, and no fair limit can be put on the people who deserve your thanks. But in this case there are two mentions that must be made: Joe Durepos, my erudite and insightful agent, who would not rest until he had pulled this book forth from me, and Marc Allen, my publisher and lifetime friend, who has always encouraged me to speak from the highest vision that is contained in my heart. In some fundamental way, this is their book, and I offer my special thanks to each of them for their unflagging efforts in bringing it to pass.

Beyond them, I must thank my immediate family — my wife, Louise, whose solid and steadfast love always offers me safe harbor, and my son, Nick, whose very presence serves as a constant reminder that life is a blessing and an honor and a joy. Thanks must also go to all the good people at New World Library, who do their work with pride and caring; and to my larger circle of friends and family who have leavened my life with their friendship, challenges, and love.

Lastly, I must pay quiet homage to this northern land on which I live, for winnowing my thoughts and giving a timbre to my vision; and to the Native people among whom I live, for reminding me that an honest voice is a humble voice, and that the earth around us, as surely as the sky above, sings the song of the spirit.

To all of you, and to those unmentioned, I hope this book finds favor in your eyes.

New World Library is dedicated to
publishing books and cassettes that inspire
and challenge us to improve the quality
of our lives and our world.

Our books and tapes are available
in bookstores everywhere.
For a catalog of our complete library
of fine books and cassettes, contact:

NEW WORLD LIBRARY
14 Pamaron Way
Novato, California 94949
Phone: (415) 884-2100
Fax: (415) 884-2199
Or call toll-free: (800) 972-6577
Catalog requests: Ext. 900
Ordering: Ext. 902

E-mail: escort@nwlib.com
http://www.nwlib.com